IMAGES
of America

THE UNITED STATES ARMY
AT FORT KNOX

This is the legendary M-4 "Sherman" tank. Armored School soldiers at Fort Knox were among the first to test this tank when it debuted in 1941. More than 49,000 Sherman tanks were produced between 1942 and 1946.

IMAGES
of America

THE UNITED STATES ARMY
AT FORT KNOX

Matthew D. Rector

ARCADIA

Copyright © 2005 by Matthew D. Rector
ISBN 0-7385-1791-7

Published by Arcadia Publishing
Charleston SC, Chicago IL, Portsmouth NH, San Francisco CA

Printed in Great Britain

Library of Congress Catalog Card Number: 2005920052

For all general information contact Arcadia Publishing at:
Telephone 843-853-2070
Fax 843-853-0044
E-mail sales@arcadiapublishing.com
For customer service and orders:
Toll-Free 1-888-313-2665

Visit us on the internet at http://www.arcadiapublishing.com

CONTENTS

ACKNOWLEDGMENTS

Since arriving in Kentucky, I have accumulated a wealth of historic photographs and items that document Fort Knox from its establishment as a camp in World War I until the present day. Many of the photographs contained in this book came from personal collections, historic Fort Knox publications, and the Patton Museum. Often my research is enhanced by the discovery of new photographs from a veteran's personal scrapbook or collection. I have had the good fortune to meet with some who have taken part and helped shape the history of Fort Knox. This book would not be possible without the assistance and contribution of many people who share my interest in the history of this important Army post. I extend my sincere thanks to Maj. Gen. Terry Tucker, Col. Keith Armstrong, Dr. Richard Helmkamp, Jessica Evans, Al Freeland, Donnie McGar, and Gary Kempf for their assistance. Thanks also to Bill Hanson, Lorraine Allen, Debbie Wallace, and Dave Thompson at the Armor School library. I thank Frank Jardim, Charles Lemons, and Candace Fuller at the Patton Museum. For their contributions, I thank Calvin Clemons, Richard Briggs, Heino Erichsen, Robert M. Fusselman, Mary Jo and James Jones, Paul Urbahns, and Joe Wilson Jr., and all of the friendly people at Fort Knox. I thank my family for always supporting my interest in history and historic preservation and, most importantly, I thank my wife, Lucy-Jane, who always supports and aids me in my projects.

A Howitzer Company marches at a review at Camp Knox in the 1920s.

FOREWORD

The military history of Fort Knox dates back to the Civil War when Union and Confederate armies bivouacked at nearby sites such as Fort Duffield. From its vantage point near the Ohio River, the region was a gateway between the North and South. Commanders back then knew the area had strategic significance. Today, Fort Knox is even more vital as the Home of Armor and U.S. Army Recruiting Command.

No doubt, soldiers have worn a lot of leather off combat boots trampling over the rugged Fort Knox terrain. The soil is red clay, and soldiers grow here better than almost anywhere else. We produce the best the Army has to offer on about 109,000 acres of Kentucky real estate bordering Hardin, Bullitt and Meade Counties.

Training Soldiers at Fort Knox is an Army tradition that began when the U.S. government bought 40,000 local acres in 1918 in the vicinity of a town named Stithton and renamed the area in honor of Maj. Gen. Henry Knox, the Chief of Artillery for the Continental Army and the nation's first secretary of war. The artillery training mission was terminated after World War I, but the military saw the future need and kept control of the region. For 10 years, from 1922 to 1932, the training area hosted Reserve and National Guard Soldiers. From 1925 to 1928, the hills were called the Camp Henry Knox National Forest.

Armor first entered the Army vocabulary in 1916 when the British introduced the tank at the Battle of Cambrai. The U.S. adopted armored warfare in the 1920s, and Congress authorized the mechanized force in 1930. The Armored Force was born on July 10, 1940, with the establishment of the Headquarters, Armor Force and the Headquarters, I Armored Corps right here at Fort Knox. Land warfare hasn't been the same since.

Now, let's get back to the mud. We train over 2,000 armor crewmen and cavalry scouts each day at Fort Knox. Another 1,000 troopers cover the fundamentals of soldiering in Basic Combat Training. The training is tough and realistic, and we wouldn't have it any other way. The main gun tubes spit out smoke and fire year-round on our ranges, and there's no shortage of cadence calling. The legendary hills, dubbed "Misery" and "Agony" by soldiers who foot marched up and down them decades ago, still lead to our vast northern range complexes. And the red-briar covered hillsides of Mount Eden continue to produce outstanding new sergeants in our Primary Leadership Development Course.

What has changed is technology and how we use it. Today, armor crewmen climb into tanks equipped with laser range finders and target acquisition computers. In fact, a completely digital complex, Wilcox Range, will open in 2005. Our soldiers already train in a mock city where they hone their skills in simulated urban combat. Meanwhile, the Unit of Action Maneuver Battle Lab at Fort Knox develops the Army's combat vehicles of the future. A couple of years ago, Fort Knox hosted selective testing of the Army's newest combat vehicle, the Stryker.

The Abrams Tank and Bradley Fighting Vehicle made their debut over 20 years ago. In support of the American Mounted Warrior, they will continue to rule the battlefield for decades to come. As the Iraqi Army can attest, the U.S. Army's Main Battle Tank has no equal on the battlefield. We intend to keep it that way.

That kind of firepower carries an awesome responsibility. The soldiers who train to fight as armor crewmen are true professionals. They are the best trained force ever to crew armored vehicles for this or any other Army. The Basic Combat Training, the Armor Crewmen and Cavalry Scout courses at Fort Knox are the best there are—bar none!

We will always keep the history and traditions of armor alive at Fort Knox. We welcome you to stop by and visit Fort Knox or the Patton Museum sometime when you're in the area. In the meantime, turn the pages, and enjoy this book, dedicated to Fort Knox, its soldiers, civilians, and our rich history.

—Terry L. Tucker, Major General, United States Army, Chief of Armor

FOREWORD

Fort Knox holds significant meaning to me personally because I've watched this installation evolve over my lifetime, from my childhood in the late 1950s to today. It is an installation rich in history and military significance—great people built it and great people maintain it today. Since being selected as the Garrison Commander, I made it a priority and take pride in the staff's efforts to revitalize the post, bringing it back to its original appearance while changing to a transforming Army.

My father trained on the grounds of Fort Knox as early as 1948, and I now finish my Army career here after a short 26 years of active duty. Training and equipment changed over the years. What once was totally focused on defeating the Soviet Union on the plains of Germany is now focused on the contemporary operating environment of Southwest Asia.

The one aspect of our Army that never changes is the soldier—better trained and equipped, our soldiers are the best in the world today. Fort Knox range and training facilities are among the best, and I've had the pleasure to lead the modernization and digitization of our facilities. Our capability, including simulation and modeling, would make those who initially trained here in 1918 stare in awe. The Zussman Urban Training Complex is a mock city built on Fort Knox in 1999 where soldiers participate in urban combat training environments and scenarios that prepare them for the battlefields of the 21st century.

Fort Knox is not here just to train soldiers. The post is a city in itself, designed to support all the needs of the community. It is a family post with homes and recreational facilities designed to provide the best quality of life for soldiers, families, and other patrons.

I have fond memories of attending school at Van Voorhis Elementary and Walker and McDonald Middle Schools; shopping at the commissary and PX, Toyland and Four Seasons; and playing "Little Tankers" youth sports. Today, the Fort Knox schools continue to teach our soldiers' children, and we provide sports activities like the ones I played many years ago. We also offer new and exciting programs that I would never have dreamed of in years past.

I remember our quarters with their gleaming hardwood floors, many of which are not even standing on the post any more. I remember our air conditioning, which was open windows, and the ceiling fan that when turned on made the curtains stand straight out from the windows as it sucked air in from the outside. My brother and I thought that was a step up in life. Today, we are moving toward the Residential Communities Initiative and housing privatization. This modernization will provide top-quality housing to America's best —Fort Knox is making continuous improvement to our quality of life.

The historic quarters in the central cantonment area are carefully preserved to keep the look they had when first constructed in the 1930s. I used to dream about living in one of those sets of quarters. Dreams do come true. I live in there now and work daily to ensure those historic buildings and all history of Fort Knox is maintained for the next 100 years, for soldiers and their families. I have had a great life in the Army, all 48 years of it, and many of my fondest memories, old and new, were formed at Fort Knox, Kentucky.

I enjoy the history of Fort Knox and I'm proud to be part of it. I hope that you will also enjoy reading about it and will plan a visit here soon.

—Keith A. Armstrong, Colonel, United States. Army, Fort Knox Garrison Commander

One
1903–1931

In 1903, a series of military maneuvers was held in West Point, Kentucky, and in communities south of that town. The temporary headquarters was named Camp Young. The United States's involvement in World War I necessitated the opening of additional training facilities for the military, and in 1918, the Army returned to the area with the intention of creating a permanent post. In that year, Camp Knox was officially designated and named after Maj. Gen. Henry Knox, chief of field artillery from 1775 to 1782, chief of staff of the Army from 1782 to 1783, and secretary of war from 1785 to 1794.

An artillery encampment in West Point was photographed in the early years of Camp Knox.

—Some of Uncle Sam's Fighting Machinery as Seen
West Point, Ky., Oct. 9th, 1903.

In this detail of a stereoview, "Some of Uncle Sam's Fighting Machinery" are depicted during military maneuvers held at West Point in October 1903.

A detail from a 1903 stereoview depicts an Army inspection in West Point. The military maneuvers lasted from September 28 through October 16, 1903. During that time, mock battles were staged between the regular Army and the Kentucky State Guard.

Pvt. Joseph Nowaki of Company F, 2nd Michigan, was one of the soldiers who participated in the 1903 military maneuvers at Camp Young in West Point, Kentucky.

The Army was especially interested in the area because of its proximity to rail lines that ran to Louisville and elsewhere. This line ran directly into what would become Camp Knox.

A car makes its way on a rustic road, possibly the Louisville and Nashville Turnpike, at Camp Knox.

Major William H. Radcliffe (1879–1952) was the constructing quartermaster at Camp Knox, and the town that developed around Camp Knox would be named after him. Major Radcliffe arrived in the small village of Stithton on July 26, 1918. The initial construction plan for Camp Knox was to accommodate a six-brigade artillery training camp along with the associated support areas. The original authorizations called for housing to be made for 60,000 men and 27,000 animals.

The Louisville, Henderson, and St. Louis Depot was a drop-off and delivery point for many of the soldiers stationed at Camp Knox. This railroad line originally went from Louisville to Henderson, Kentucky, but had been extended to St. Louis by the time the Army arrived.

An artillery crew drills near the Camp Knox cantonment in West Point. Artillery commander Gen. Dwight E. Aultman came to Camp Knox in 1919 and served as Post Commander.

West Point was the location of artillery camps into the 1920s. This particular photograph of artillery limbers was taken near the location of the West Point brickyard.

Camp Knox soldiers prepare for an artillery drill near West Point. Most likely taken after World War I, this photograph may depict members of the Third Field Artillery who came to Camp Knox 1921.

The vast number of soldiers who were stationed at West Point began to disrupt daily life and prompted Army authorities to declare martial law. Lt. Col. J.B.W. Corey became acting mayor of the small river town.

An artillery crew in action is the subject of this photograph taken at Camp Knox. The artillery range at Camp Knox became famous for it seven-mile range along a three-mile front. This range was often praised and spoken of by artillery officers around the country.

This bird's-eye view shows the first barracks at Camp Knox. America's continued involvement in World War I made it necessary to establish and build the new installation at Camp Knox swiftly. Major construction of the post concentrated in the area of Stithton, Kentucky, a small farming community.

Standardized plans were used to build most of these World War I mobilization buildings, and identical structures could be found on most other installations around the country. In this era and region of the country, horse-drawn equipment was still regularly used along with automobiles.

Captain Lewis and Second Lieutenant Mitchell are picture with their squad of anti-aircraft gunners in this photograph from the early 1920s.

Soldiers stand around an unidentified building in Stithton. Many of the town's buildings were demolished to make room for standardized military structures.

18

An American flag is raised at Camp Knox. "Work progressed in all branches utilizing ever[y] available day light hour for seven days a week until the signing of the armistice," Maj. W.H. Radcliffe, constructing quartermaster at Camp Knox, wrote in his completion report in September 1919.

The Military Police Headquarters at Camp Knox was first located in one of Stithton's former residences. Many of the houses in the town were utilized for the Army's purposes. Modest Victorian architecture once occupied by Stithton residents became homes used by Army officers and their families.

The Hostess House, also known as the Guest or Visitor's House, was constructed with funds raised by the National Catholic War Council in 1919. Built for $50,000, it was considered one of the finest buildings at Camp Knox. It was later used as the post hospital and, during World War II, was headquarters for the 1st Armored "Old Ironsides" Division.

Mule-drawn wagons still delivered the mail in the early days at Camp Knox. In this photograph of the first post office at Camp Knox, soldiers take a break by a mail wagon.

Infantrymen drill at Camp Knox. In the early 1920s, the Army's force was reduced, and in 1922, it was deemed necessary to close the post as a permanent installation. Although closed by use of the regular Army, Camp Knox remained an active training center for Army programs. Between 1925 and 1928, the area was designated as Camp Henry Knox National Forest until two infantry companies were assigned to the post.

Barracks and warehouses built to accommodate the growing soldier population during and after World War I were taken from standardized plans. Such plans were used to construct most of these World War I mobilization buildings, and identical buildings could be found on most other installations around the country.

A cavalryman clears an obstacle while training. Numerous cavalry units passed through and trained at Camp Knox in the 1930s.

For many soldiers at Camp Knox, the train depot was the first and last building they saw. This depot was used throughout the 1920s.

A typical street scene at Camp Knox included unpaved roads and wooden barracks. This photo from the early 1920s depicts an unknown street on the post.

The first movie theater was constructed to resemble a typical frontier fort. Silent films would be shown at this theater for the soldiers' amusement.

The headquarters building was much like the other buildings on the post, unassuming and constructed according to standardized plans.

24

An airfield has been located at Camp Knox since its creation. Accidents were not an uncommon occurrence in the early years of flight.

It is noted that two crewmen died in the crash photographed above. In 1938, construction of a new airfield named Godman Army Air Field began.

This is the officers' mess hall for the 81st Field Artillery. This unit started out in World War I as the 22nd and 23rd Cavalry Regiments. The need for additional artillery units in Europe prompted these two cavalry regiments to convert to artillery. At Camp Knox, the 81st Field Artillery was eventually designated as the 4th and 5th Field Artillery Training Batteries.

The new Dixie Highway through Camp Knox allowed for easier travel to area towns like West Point and Elizabethtown.

YOUNG AMERICA

Camp Knox and Fort Knox were the sites for the 5th Corps Area Citizens' Military Training Camp (CMTC) from 1921 to 1940. The CMTC was an Army-sponsored program that allowed young men to receive military training for one month during the summers.

Newly arrived CMTC candidates pose for a photo in the 1920s taken at a rail station at Camp Knox. Transportation to the camp was paid for or reimbursed by the war department, under various conditions.

Colonel Joseph F. Gohn (1873–1959) welcomes new candidates to Camp Knox's CMTC.

The civilian training quarters pictured here may have been used by one of the various military training programs held at Camp Knox.

After World War I, Camp Knox was used by reserve officer training, the United States Army National Guard, and Citizens' Military Training Camps. Existing barracks continued to be utilized.

The mess hall for CMTC candidates mimicked those found at active Army posts of the day.

Two CMTC candidates prepare a mess hall before a feast that included fried chicken and watermelon.

A color guard on parade is photographed in a familiar scene recreated at other CMTC camps. In the CMTC program's first six years of existence, over 158,000 men were trained. Most CMTC candidates only attended one year, although it was possible to attend four straight years.

CMTC cadets exercise every morning as part of their daily calisthenics.

Outside the barracks, the CMTC 5th Corps Area was comprised of men from Indiana, Kentucky, Ohio, and West Virginia. The 5th Corps Area was the first in the country to allow high school credits for those who attended camp.

CMTC candidates on cook and fatigue duty take time out for a photograph.

Various athletic activities were planned every day at the post. A candidate had a variety of sports from which to choose. A champion baseball team poses in this photograph.

Capt. Howard Clark, commanding officer, and Peter F. McCormick, band leader, led the CMTC Band in the summer of 1924. Most camps had at least one band and at times included an orchestra.

Citizens of all classes and backgrounds could be found at the CMTC at Camp Knox. Pulitzer Prize–winning author and poet Robert Penn Warren penned his first poem at Camp Knox as a 17-year-old CMTC candidate in 1922.

Maj. Gen. Robert L. Howze (1864–1926) commanded the 5th Corps Area. Howze was a Medal of Honor recipient and was the first commander of the 1st Cavalry Division, from 1921 to 1925.

In reference to luxurious train car, soldiers named their vehicles "Army Pullmans." Safety was not one of the top concerns when traveling to different areas on the post in the early years of Camp Knox.

A pontoon bridge is constructed and implemented over a lake by CMTC candidates.

CMTC candidates pause to eat a meal while marching. By 1925, Camp Knox had become the largest military reservation in the United States. With around 33,000 acres, the reservation was often cited for its scenic hills and rugged terrain.

After their one month in camp, CMTC candidates file past their commanders in one last review.

An artist among the Reserve Officers' Training Corps (ROTC) cadets at Camp Knox created this comical feature for their yearbook, *The Guidon*.

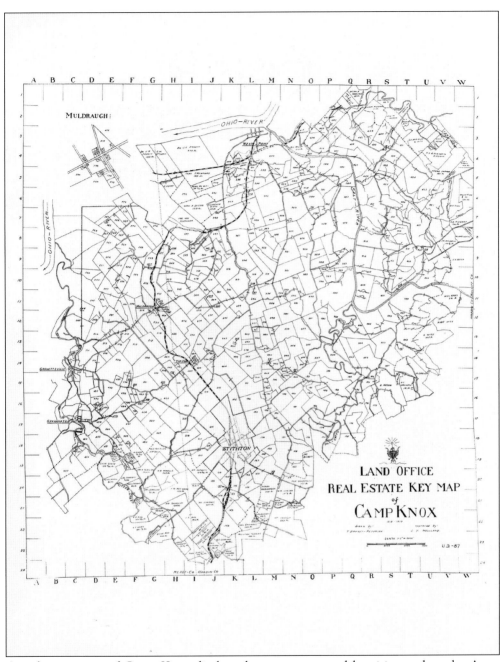

A real estate map of Camp Knox displays the property owned by citizens when the Army arrived. The citizens who owned those tracts were forced to find new homes. Some moved to neighboring counties only to have their land purchased by the Army in subsequent land acquisitions in the 1940s and 1950s.

An artillery piece is fired in a Memorial Day salute at Camp Knox.

Camp Knox soldiers pile into an Army truck in this photograph taken around 1924.

A non-commissioned officer stands next to a group of civilian workers at the Camp Knox post office in the 1920s.

These two women worked at the Hostess House at Camp Knox around 1925. They catered to soldiers and their visiting families to make their stay on the post a memorable one.

Soldiers standing on a newly constructed pontoon bridge pause for a photograph. Citizens, observing the activities of the day, are visible on the far side of the lake with their vehicles,.

When this photograph was taken in 1924, CMTC candidates were required to know how horse-drawn artillery operated.

Mounted officers and standing citizens watch from their reviewing stand a final review by CMTC candidates.

The Officer's Club was an imposing structure at Camp Knox in 1926.

It was common for CMTC candidates skilled in art to create drawings for their yearbook, *The Mess Kit*. Here, one grumbles about the hardships but appreciates the opportunity to return the next year.

44

Two

1932–1940

Upon the recommendation of Lt. Col. Adna R. Chaffee Jr. and Col. Daniel Van Voorhis, Camp Knox was chosen to be the new headquarters for the mechanized cavalry. The size and terrain of Camp Knox made this a suitable area for such training. On January 1, 1932, Camp Knox was made a permanent installation once again, and since then, it has been known as Fort Knox. Two weeks later, the 1st Cavalry Regiment, the Army's oldest mounted unit, arrived at Fort Knox and exchanged its horses for armored combat cars.

The main cantonment was constructed between 1933 and 1940. Most of the buildings were constructed from standardized plans, designed in a Georgian Colonial Revival style, created by the Army Quartermaster Corps. The architecture and planning of this area is typical of a permanent Army post in the years before World War II.

Chaffee Avenue led directly to the flagpole and into the heart of the main cantonment at Fort Knox.

This photograph of the administration building was taken before it was officially completed on November 2, 1934. The building took almost one year to complete at a cost of $67,112.65. This building is more commonly known as the headquarters building.

The new administration building and flagpole were built using the same contract. Fort Knox was destined to play a vital role in the development of Army military tactics, doctrine, and equipment. In this 1934 photograph, guards stand at attention while signs of new permanent construction surround them.

An M2A4 tank travels down an unidentified road at Fort Knox. With a crew of four men, this tank was armed with a 37 mm gun and eight 76 mm machine guns.

Soldiers learn how to operate an M1917A1 .30 caliber water-cooled machine gun. Developed by John Browning, this machine gun was used by the Army into the 1950s.

Construction on a new hospital began in 1933 during the first construction phase at Fort Knox. It was completed in 1935 at a cost of nearly $171,000.

In 1940, during the second phase of permanent construction at Fort Knox, another wing was added to the hospital.

The 1937 flooding of the Ohio River briefly stalled construction of the theater. Supply houses in Louisville were unable to deliver the necessary materials for construction until March. Construction of the theater was completed in June 1937.

Among the first films to be shown in the theater were *Thunder in the City*, *Maytime*, and *The Frame Up*.

The new movie theater contained ample seating along with lounges, toilet rooms, and an office—everything "required for a modern theatre," according to its compilation report.

Fort Knox Theatre

FORT KNOX THEATRE

The architecture of the theater coincided with the other buildings on the post. The standardized plans used to construct this building were also utilized at other Army posts at that time.

Housing for officers was a top priority during the first construction phase. This May 1934 photograph depicts field officers' quarters under construction.

This postcard illustrates the attractive quarters available to officers and their families at Fort Knox.

In 1994, it was determined that the Fort Knox Cantonment Historic District was eligible for listing on the National Register of Historic Places (NRHP).

SINGLE NON-COMMISSIONED OFFICERS' QTRS looking NORTHWEST on A STREET. Nov. 1, 1934.

Only one street at Fort Knox featured houses constructed in this style for single non-commissioned officers. Like many of the other housing plans, the design of these houses could be seen at other posts.

The commanding general's quarters displayed slight architectural differences to distinguish it from the other housing. This photograph was taken when Maj. Gen. Adna Chaffee, the Father of Armor and Cavalry, occupied the quarters.

Housing plans varied on the post. The duplex houses shown here were constructed for field officers and their families.

Some field officers' quarters were single units. Many of the houses and barracks on the post were roofed with attractive clay tile shingles.

A group of newly constructed houses sit by an unpaved road on the post. The houses photographed here were for non-commissioned soldiers and their families.

Works Progress Administration (WPA) workers remodel a house remaining from the extinct town of Stithton.

Quarters T-72 was also a remnant of Stithton. The "T" in front of the building number stood for "temporary." This building may have lasted up to the end of World War II, but was probably demolished soon after.

The Post Chapel is one of the oldest and most prominent buildings to exist at Fort Knox. Built in 1899, the chapel was originally constructed as St. Patrick's Church for Stithton residents. The Army first used it as a theater until the new theater was constructed. The church was then returned to its original function.

This photograph shows the first entrance to Fort Knox as it was being built in 1935. Note the new lampposts and streets.

Located near the entrance of Fort Knox, the Post Exchange contained stores providing various services for residents on the post. Services included a watch repair shop and a photo studio.

The Wiseman Building may possibly pre-date Camp Knox, although its exact construction date is uncertain. The signs on the exterior display the various shops located within.

A scout car is pictured during a review of the 7th Cavalry Brigade around the old Stithton circle near the entrance to Fort Knox.

Yeomans Hall was originally built for nearly $62,000 as bachelor officers' quarters (BOQ) in 1934. The two-story porte-cochère, supported by four columns, is a character-defining element of this building.

Works Progress Administration camps also performed work at Fort Knox. One of the most notable and necessary buildings constructed at Fort Knox, the water filtration plant, was a WPA project.

The water filtration plant was built in the Art Deco style and stands out among the traditional Georgian Colonial Revival style found in the other buildings on the post. Completed in 1938, the structure displays waterfall motifs in the walls.

The post school was constructed in 1939 to accommodate additional units arriving at Fort Knox in the late 1930s. The building was designed in the prevalent Georgian Colonial Revival style and contains a unique feature at Fort Knox, a copper-domed bell tower.

The fire and guard house was completed in 1935 at a cost of approximately $64,500. This building is still used as a fire station at Fort Knox.

The Noncommissioned Officers' Club was built as a WPA project and featured a rustic interior that included exposed timber.

The completed Noncommissioned Officers' Club included a pool for soldiers and their families. This building survived into the 1990s before it was demolished.

Concrete is poured for a road in front of partially completed barracks. Labor was supplied under the provisions of the National Industrial Recovery Act, and various local contractors were used.

The three images shown in this postcard display various panoramic views of the new permanent construction at Fort Knox.

The four company barracks pictured were actually massed in one structure.

A photograph of the barracks displays the four wings projecting from the rear.

The enlisted barracks were constructed on a mammoth scale. These barracks were 3.5 stories high and 455 feet long.

Various cars were photographed along with the rear of one of the newly completed barracks.

A new Officers' Mess was constructed in 1934.

This photograph provides a view of the Officers' Club that was constructed during the time period of Camp Knox.

A field house was constructed at Fort Knox to cater to the recreational needs of the growing population on the post.

Two water towers were erected in 1935 and 1937 near the post school and became landmarks on the post.

A combat car in the mechanized cavalry tests the waters near an old homestead at Fort Knox.

A scout car and equipment are moved across a river during a muddy Fort Knox training exercise.

A youthful soldier holds a horse's bridle during the 2nd Army maneuvers at Fort Knox in 1936. This scene would be increasingly rare as units traded in their horses for armored vehicles and tanks.

A battery of 75 Howitzers are lined up in this postcard view. The 75 Howitzer could be disassembled to allow for easy transportation over difficult terrain.

The United States Bullion Depository was constructed on property set aside by Fort Knox. The director of the mint, the United States Treasury, was placed in charge of the depository. It received its first shipment of gold in 1937 under the security of the 7th Cavalry Brigade.

In addition to gold, the depository has stored important documents including the Declaration of Independence, the United States Constitution, the Articles of Confederation, Lincoln's Gettysburg Address, Lincoln's second inaugural address, three volumes of the Gutenberg Bible, and the Magna Carta.

Gold is loaded onto trucks from the railway at Fort Knox.

A scout car leads a group of trucks that have just picked up a shipment of gold destined for the Bullion Depository.

Full Field Inspection.

Fort Knox soldiers stand at attention in front of their tents for a full field inspection.

Tank in Armored Force Division

Civilians stand among soldiers from the Armored Force Division to observe a tank exercise.

Three
1941–1945

On July 10, 1940, in partial response to the war in Europe, the Army established the Armored Force, which is headquartered at Fort Knox. As a result of the Selective Service program, thousands of new military personnel come to Fort Knox. The military reservation, even with almost 1,000 buildings, was forced to accommodate the new soldiers in tent cities. A new construction boom occurred to build facilities for the large numbers of arriving men. As a result of the mobilization, almost 3,000 additional buildings were constructed during World War II.

A tank crew poses on Brooks Field with the contents that go inside a tank. The headquarters building at Fort Knox can be viewed at the left of the photograph. The Armored Force School and Replacement Training Center were activated on October 1, 1940. Later that month, the name was changed to the Armored Force Replacement Center.

With the Japanese attack on Pearl Harbor, Hawaii, the United States of America entered World War II. On December 8, 1941, Pfc. Robert H. Brooks was killed during an aerial assault on the island of Luzon and became the first World War II battle casualty of the Armored Force. The main parade ground at Fort Knox was dedicated in his name.

With the explosion of new recruits arriving at Fort Knox, there was an imminent need to construct "temporary" barracks. Many soldiers slept in tents as they waited for the barracks to be completed.

Future "Armoraiders" arrive at Fort Knox by rail and are greeted by officers at the reception center who immediately take a roll call.

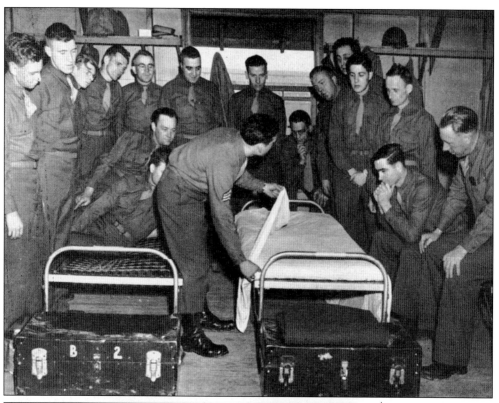

A sergeant instructs new recruits on ways to keep their barracks tidy. Some of the following photographs illustrate what some new soldiers could expect at Fort Knox.

New recruits are pictured singing and playing instruments in this photograph.

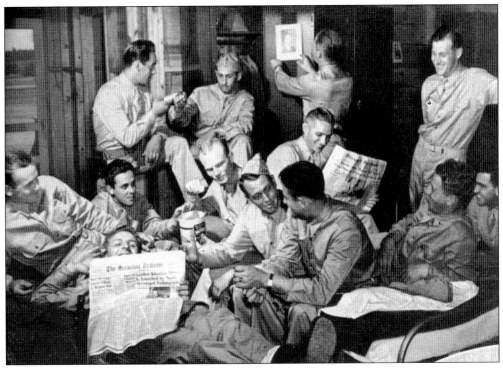

Recruits get comfortable in their new barracks.

Some soldiers pass the time by reading newspapers and magazines. The thoughts of the soldier in the forefront of this photograph are only known to him.

In this photograph, soldiers are issued field gear before field exercises.

During their fifth week of basic training, soldiers find themselves on the firing line.

Recruits get their first peek at a tank at the Armored Force Replacement Center. The center officially became known as the Armored Force Replacement Training Center (AFRTC) in April 1941. The AFRTC continued to grow, prompting another name change in 1943 to the Armor Replacement Training Center (ARTC). Due to the increase in enrollment, a two-shift day was required. The school reached its peak of approximately 9,000 students on January 29, 1943.

A trainee is instructed on how to use an MI rocket launcher. This anti-tank gun usually needed a two-man crew—one man to serve as a gunner and the other to reload. Resembling a musical instrument made famous by radio comedian Bob Burns, soldiers commonly referred to this gun as a bazooka.

The quote accompanying this public relations photo states, "Then comes chow! He takes his mess kit and stands in line in front of the mess tent, eagerly awaiting the hot food."

A Retreat Ceremony is captured on a rainy day in this 1941 photograph. The post hospital is located on the other side of Brooks Field.

The M2A1 Half Track was a personnel carrier that combined features of a truck and a tank. It was armed with .50 caliber gun.

A soldier identified as Floyd McQueen salutes as he sits upon a motorcycle. Harley Davidson and Indian motorcycle companies produced thousands of motorcycles for the Army during World War II.

Soldiers at Fort Knox ride in a rare 1940 Bantam BRC 60 Jeep, often hailed as the second oldest jeep model. Only 70 were made by American Bantam Car Company of Butler, Pennsylvania.

Armored Force Radio Scout Car

This postcard illustrates two radio operators in a half track that is used as a radio scout car.

On July 25, 1940, Elizabethtown, Kentucky, native Mary Josephine (Richerson) Jones began working at Fort Knox as a stenographer. In 1944, she accepted a position with the state department and soon was sent to Rome, Italy, to work in the American embassy as a cryptographer. She returned to Fort Knox in the summer of 1945. This photo of her was taken by the Army Signal Corps in 1940 for public relations purposes.

From left to right, Martha Shelton, Mary Gene Miller, Mary Jo Richerson, and Irene Pittman stand in front of their quarters in building T-42. T-42 was a surviving house from the community of Stithton. The residents printed their own newsletter, appropriately titled *Tea Four Two: The House of Utter Confusion*. Many citizens who worked on the post were quartered in houses or dormitories.

From left to right, Martha Shelton, Bea Dickerson, Annetta Jane Mason, Irene Pittman, and Eleanor Stevenson pose for this photograph in winter at Fort Knox. Some of them proudly wear new fur coats purchased with their earnings from jobs on the post.

One of the few permanent buildings at Fort Knox to depart from the Colonial Georgian Revival style architecture was the Officers' Country Club. The design of the building was modified from a ship pattern.

Officers Country Club

Completed in 1940 by the WPA, the Officers' Country Club was built next to Lindsey Golf Course. The stone wall constructed near the building was also built by the WPA.

The Officers' Club was completed with the addition of a swimming pool. The empty pool was photographed in January 1941.

Soldiers stand out in front of Fort Knox's A & R Restaurant, which catered to residents and soldiers on the post in the 1940s.

In this posed photograph, newly arrived ladies from the Women's Army Auxiliary Corps, better known as WAACs, are photographed receiving immediate attention from GIs at Fort Knox.

WAACs were the first women to serve in the Army in functions other than that of nurses. They performed a variety of tasks, allowing more men to serve in combat roles.

WAACs line up for dinner at a mess hall at Fort Knox. WAACs dine in a separate mess hall from the Armored School soldiers.

In the summer of 1943, the WAAC was converted into the Women's Army Corps (WAC). The number of women who served in the WAAC and the WAC exceeded 150,000. WACs remained at Fort Knox into the 1950s.

The addition of new housing at Fort Knox during World War II prompted the press to nickname the post "Boomtown." Only 864 buildings existed on the post in July 1940. By August 1943, there were close to 3,820 buildings. New land was also purchased, bringing the total acreage to 106, 861.

Two-story wooden barracks were quickly constructed to house the thousands of trainees passing through the Armor School. While considered temporary and only expected to last for the duration of the war, these barracks were used at Fort Knox into the 21st century.

The housing area known as "Goldville" was occupied by married soldiers stationed on the post. Sgt. Robert M. Fusselman and his wife resided in the housing seen here.

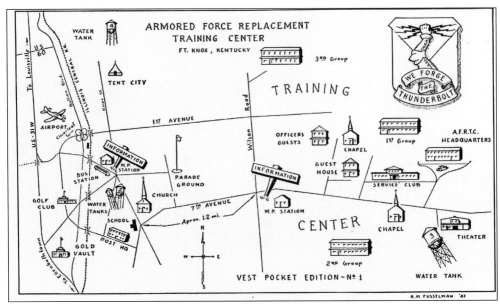

Staff Sgt. Robert M. Fusselman (below) designed this postcard for new recruits arriving to the Armored Force Replacement Training Center. Fusselman was an architecture student at Ohio State University when he was drafted in 1941. After his basic training, he was instructed to design many of the training aids and various new buildings on the post. He left Fort Knox in 1945 and was sent to both the European and Pacific theaters of the war.

Staff Sgt. Robert M. Fusselman was instructed by Maj. Morris "Buddy" Benz to design a new library for the Armored Force School. Soldiers detailed on construction duty pose in front of the new library.

Known as library number two, the new library featured a stone fireplace and exterior stonework. Much of the structure was built with recycled lumber from barracks and existing farm structures on the reservation.

The leading lyric soprano for the Metropolitan Opera, Suzanne Fischer (1903–1990), gets a tour of a tank. A native of West Virginia, Fischer debuted at the Metropolitan Opera in 1935.

Bing Crosby (1903–1907) meets Commanding Gen. Jacob L. Devers before putting on a show for the troops at Fort Knox. Crosby was a favorite performer on USO tours.

Three soldiers comically pose for a photographer during their basic training at Fort Knox.

OX AND ASS, CAMEL AND PEEP, CHRISTMAS AT FT. KNOX, KY., 1942

Fort Knox's version of a manger scene was photographed for a postcard entitled, "Ox and Ass, Camel and Peep, Christmas at Ft. Knox, KY., 1942."

The LST building was constructed on a non-standard plan in 1942 and was designed by the United States Navy specifically to resemble the well deck of a Landing Ship Tank (LST) transport. The significance of the LST building is based on its critical role in the development of the large amphibious landing ships that were crucial to the Allied war effort in World War II. This building represents the first and only time that the United States Navy constructed such a large, full-scale mockup to investigate crucial ship design.

Maj. Gen. Jacob L. Devers, Commanding General of the Armored Force, inspects the LST mock up. Immediately following the Navy's use of the structure for engineering studies, the building was given to the Army for their use.

This is a view of the interior bay of the LST building with tanks in position. Following World War II, the structure served a number of on-going training functions including a trainee classroom and a night vision training facility. Today, the building is used as an exhibit hall for many of the armored vehicles in the Patton Museum's collection.

This view of the control room for the LST building shows the telephone switch board and net control crew. Twenty-three telephones were required for intercommunication.

This photograph depicts the Honor Guard forming up for the arrival of President Franklin Delano Roosevelt at Fort Knox on April 28, 1943.

On April 28, 1943, President Roosevelt visited Fort Knox. In this photo, President Roosevelt is given an Armored Force School souvenir.

President Roosevelt and Maj. Gen. Jacob L. Devers converse as they are reviewed by the Armored Force School. Devers (1887–1979) succeeded Maj. Gen. Adna Chaffee in August 1941 as Fort Knox's Post Commander. At age 54, he was the youngest major general in the Army's land forces. He left Fort Knox in 1943 to lead the 6th Army across Europe during World War II.

President Roosevelt is accompanied by Fort Knox Post Commander Maj. Gen. Jacob L. Devers at a tank range where they witness training.

A tough customer in camouflage uniform.

A "tough customer in camouflage uniform" poses in this photograph from the Armor School. Camouflage uniforms were rare in the U.S. Army. The Marines used these uniforms more in the Pacific Theater of Operations during World War II.

Soldiers fire their M1 Garand rifles at an unknown range at Fort Knox. The M1 Garand rifle came in to production in 1936 and was used extensively by the Army until it was replaced by the M14 and M16 rifles in the 1960s.

An AFRTC Jeep driver goes airborne in this photograph.

Soldiers of the 8th Armored Division wait to board trains. The 8th Armored Division was activated at Fort Knox on April 1, 1942, served as a training division, and was also known as the official guardian of the Gold Vault. It left Fort Knox for Fort Campbell in February 1943.

The M-7 Self-Propelled Howitzer was based on the M4 tank and included an anti-aircraft machine gun.

Thirteen weeks into basic training, these soldiers learn about urban warfare in "Little Tokyo." The village was constructed to simulate the environment they might see when deployed.

Soldiers are met by explosions outside Little Tokyo. The village was used for training into the Vietnam Conflict era.

Sv. Hunter - Ft. Knox Ky

Fort Knox enlistee John Hunter is photographed during a fatigue detail. He sent the next few photographs home to his family in West Virginia. On the back of this photograph, he wrote, "This was taken in my work clothes."

The photos in this grouping were found at an auction. The history and fate of John Hunter remain a mystery at the time of publication. Like John Hunter, many soldiers sent photographs home to their family. Today, these photographs are often found for sale. While unknown to the buyer, they provide a visual documentation of a personal history at Fort Knox.

This photograph illustrates officers and other soldiers taking a break from training to eat. The officers hold standard issue mess gear.

Here is another photo of John Hunter taken during field exercises. He wrote on the back of the photograph that it was taken in October 1940.

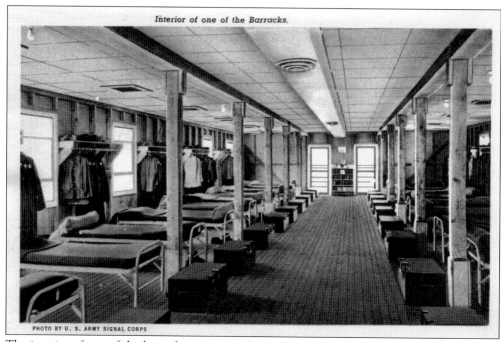

The interior of one of the barracks was a popular postcard for soldiers to send back home.

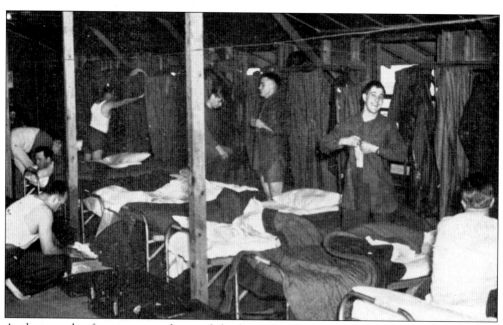

A photograph of an interior of one of the barracks illustrates the crowded conditions that existed at time. Armored Force soldiers were required to be out of bed at 5 a.m.

The publicity office of the AFRTC took an active role in promoting Fort Knox and the AFRTC by publishing photographs and books. Many of the photographs found in this chapter can be credited to photographers from this office. In all probability, the unidentified officer and enlisted soldiers in this photograph worked in this office.

Attractive housing for noncommissioned officers gave the post a friendly atmosphere and sense of community.

Mary Jo and James A. Jones are photographed on their wedding day in the historic post chapel at Fort Knox in July 1946. James had just received orders for his deployment to the Far East. Mary Jo worked on the post and James was aid de camp to the Post Commander.

Lt. James A. Jones, aid to Gen. Hugh Gaffey, came to Fort Knox in September 1945. A native of Georgia, James was a seasoned veteran who had seen combat in Germany.

The caption with this photograph that appeared in an AFRTC pamphlet stated, "Then, every once in awhile a girl-friend of his shows up. And, man! Is he proud as he escorts her around the AFRTC!" Single women working on the post rarely had a difficult time finding a date when they wanted one.

Armored Force officers and some WACs spent a night on the town, arm in arm. The USO club in Radslipp was a popular dating venue.

In February 1944, Italian prisoners of war (POWs) were brought to Fort Knox's Axis prisoners of war camp. After Italy's position changed in World War II, they were allowed more freedom on the post. They were given American uniforms to wear with a patch that read "ITALY." Italian prisoners, above, are seen purchasing items from the POW canteen.

German POWs, many of whom were former members of the Afrika Korps, arrived in the late spring of 1944. The original caption accompanying this photo stated, "German prisoners prefer as little clothing as the 'law' allows, as is shown in this mess hall scene. As soon as they return from work details, they strip to shorts and shirts, and spend their spare time acquiring suntans. The mess sergeant in this mess was proud of the job he does in feeding 742 men several meals a day but declined to have his name or picture published."

The original caption for this photograph stated, "Baking bread, rolls and cakes for 724 men is a major operation at the German prisoner of war camp, and Major John L. Warrick, above, is shown inspecting the bakery where huge cinnamon rolls are coming out of the oven. Prisoners operate the bakery as well as other facilities of the prisoner of war camp." Heino Erichsen is on the right pulling the rolls from the oven. He was captured in 1943 while serving in the Afrika Korps and was first sent to POW Camp Hearne in Texas before coming to Fort Knox in the spring of 1944. He later returned to settle in America in the early 1950s and became a United States citizen.

Axis prisoners of war wait to board trains to depart from Fort Knox in the spring of 1946. These prisoners were then sent to Great Britain or France to work before being allowed to return home. They are depicted wearing United States Army-issued winter coats that have been dyed black and stenciled with the letters "P" and "W".

Mess hall workers at the post hospital are pictured here.

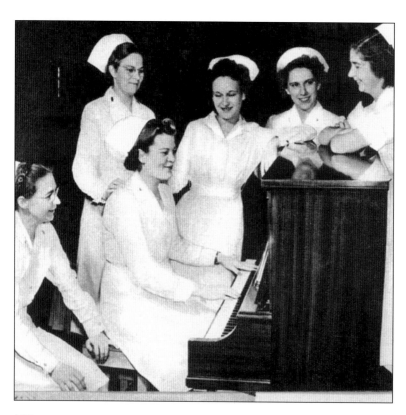

Nurses at the hospital take a break from their busy schedule to sing by the piano.

A tree located in front of the "Brick Club" is weighed down by ice. Today, the building is known as the Leader's Club and serves Army personnel and civilians of all rank.

A curious youth cautiously looks into the bowels of a giant British tank from the First World War.

Armored Force trainees find themselves working on their tank on a cold winter day in the Kentucky hills.

Various field tasks are performed by Armored Force trainees. One is seen holding his mess kit while another appears to be working on his carbine.

An officer in the Armor School assumes the gunner's position at a .30 caliber M1919 machine gun. Unlike the M1917 water-cooled machine gun, the M1919 was air cooled and much lighter.

In 1942, photographer Alfred Palmer documented training at Fort Knox for the Office of War Information (OWI). This well-known photograph depicts an M-4 tank crew.

Palmer captured M-3 tanks in action as they trained at Fort Knox.

The OWI captioned this photograph, "Infantryman with halftrack, a young soldier of the armed forces, holds and sights his Garand rifle like an old timer."

This is an M-3 tank covered with dust and dirt.

Sherman tanks roll past the post flag staff. At the end of World War II, 11,607 officers, 11,601 officer candidates, and 67,164 enlisted men graduated from the Armored School.

Four
1946–1958

On July 15, 1947, the replacement center at Fort Knox, Kentucky, was named the 3rd Armored Division. Between 1947 and 1955, more than 300,000 soldiers were trained by the division before being sent to permanent stations and units. Under the Army Reorganization Act, cavalry and armor were joined to form a new armor branch in 1950.

The Armor School entrance is guarded by two M-26 Pershing medium tanks.

A post–World War II view of the traffic circle shows the addition of a tank. The Wiseman Building is seen in the background.

This early aerial was taken looking southeast past the traffic circle.

Numerous permanent buildings were constructed on the post to house and facilitate an ever-expanding training mission. Additional land purchased in Bullitt County in the early 1950s brought the total acreage of the reservation to over 109,000.

New and improved "hammerhead barracks," designed by a Louisville architecture firm, are constructed on the post to improve living conditions for soldiers. World War II wooden barracks continued to remain in use, however.

In 1949, the Patton Museum opened in a wooden World War II mobilization building and remained there until a new museum was constructed in 1972. The museum houses a diverse and large collection of armored vehicles, which are found on interior and exterior displays.

The Patton Museum boasts an impressive collection of historical material relating to cavalry and armor, including personal items once belonging to Gen. George S. Patton Jr.

In the early 1950s, New Gordon Station, Fort Knox's tallest building, was constructed. In this photograph, Superintendent Edmund Richerson hands Deputy Post Commander Col. Stephen N. Slaughter the first stamp purchased at the New Gordon Station Post Office. On the right, Postmaster J. Wayne Hargan observes.

Soldiers at Fort Knox were not the only ones to receive new housing accommodations. New family housing was constructed on the post in the 1950s and 1960s. Named for the senators who introduced legislation for this new family housing, Capehart-Wherry Housing provided nearly 250,000 new units on Army posts around the country.

Tank commander Sgt. Joseph Wilson photographed his friends in the 758th Tank Battalion at Fort Knox while the Army was still segregated.

The Truman administration intended segregation in the Army to end in 1948. It was not implemented immediately, however. In this photograph from the early 1950s, soldiers in the 3rd Armor Division study the .30 caliber light machine gun.

Noncommissioned officers from the 3rd Armored Division are photographed in the field with their commander.

Soldiers in the 3rd Armor Division test the .30 caliber light machine gun at a firing range at Fort Knox.

The United States participated in the Korean War between Communist and non-Communist forces in Korea from 1950 to 1953. After years of heavy casualties, a cease fire ensued at the 38th parallel, where it remains to this day. During this time, the Army began production on the M-48 "Patton" tank to upgrade the M-4 "Sherman" tank. Hastened by Cold War tensions, the new tank was fielded in 1953. The M-48 carried a 90 mm gun and still exists in armies of some nations even today.

Fort Knox has contributed to the evolution of the armored tank. During the 1950s, soldiers still relied on older tanks to assist in training.

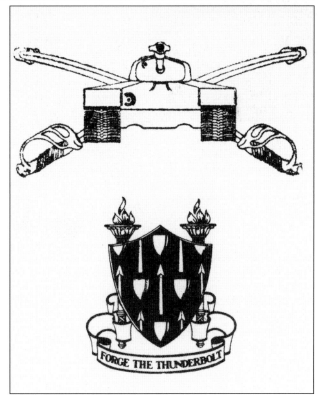

The armor insignia and device for the Armored School were designed at Fort Knox. In January 1951, armor insignia was authorized by the Department of the Army. The crossed sabers cavalry insignia and modern armor insignia were combined to represent the transition from cavalry to armor. In 1948, the device for the Armor School was approved by the Department of the Army. The escutcheons and javelins are symbolic of defensive and offensive armor, while the torches represent learning and leadership.

In 1957, visitors to Fort Knox were greeted by a new welcome monument on Muldraugh Hill, located just south of West Point, Kentucky. Since the years after World War II, Fort Knox has been instrumental in introducing new armor, such as the M-48 Patton tank, M-60, M-1 Abrams and M-2/M-3 Bradley tanks and, most recently, the newest armored vehicle known as the "Stryker." During the Cold War, the number of new soldiers instructed at the Fort Knox Training Center surpassed one million. In 1992, the United States Army Recruiting Command Headquarters relocated to Fort Knox. The headquarters is responsible for worldwide recruiting and provides the command, control, and staff support to the recruiting force. The Army now recruits more than 75,000 new soldiers annually. Today, Fort Knox continues to provide the United States Army with trained soldiers in support of Operations Noble Eagle, Enduring Freedom, and Iraqi Freedom and the Global War on Terror. In the years following the establishment of Camp Knox in 1918, Fort Knox played—and continues to play—a proud role as America's "Home of the Armor and Cavalry."